THE
EIGHTEENTH
PRESIDENCY!

WALT WHITMAN

THE
EIGHTEENTH
PRESIDENCY!

A CRITICAL TEXT EDITED BY

EDWARD F. GRIER

UNIVERSITY OF KANSAS PRESS
LAWRENCE, KANSAS

PREFACE

The purpose of this edition is to offer a complete and correct critical text of Walt Whitman's tract, "The Eighteenth Presidency!," written in 1856 but apparently never published by him except in the form of printers' proof sheets. There have been three significant editions of "The Eighteenth Presidency!" before the present one. The first was a French translation by Sylvia Beach and Adrienne Monnier from original proof sheets supplied by Jean Catel, the great pioneer of Whitman studies in France. This translation appeared in a Parisian little magazine, *Le Navire d'Argent* (III, 99-125) in March, 1926. The second, by Catel himself and in English, appeared in a limited edition at Montpellier in 1928. In the same year Clifton Joseph Furness included the tract in *Walt Whitman's Workshop,* a collection of unpublished Whitman manuscripts. Under such circumstances some justification of another edition is required other than the occasion of the hundredth anniversary of the tract.

All three previous editions, however, have serious defects. The Beach-Monnier translation, although it it very good as far as I am able to judge, is only a translation and is, moreover, very difficult to obtain. The Catel edition not only is difficult to obtain, but also has the defect of six variations (including the omission of the next-to-last sentence) from the proof sheets I have examined. These variations might possibly have been authorized by Catel's proof sheets, which contained Whitman's directions to the printer (*Le*

Navire d'Argent, III, 3), but the Beach-Monnier translation does not show them. The Furness edition, which is extremely faulty, contains forty-two errors of various kinds: misreadings, subheads run into the text, subheads and sentences (the last two) omitted. Therefore a new edition, with full introduction and notes, seems justified, and the fortunate availability of two hitherto unstudied sets of proof sheets, containing Whitman's corrections, in the collection of Mr. Charles E. Feinberg, gives a new edition an added interest.

The "original" of the "The Eighteenth Presidency!" is a two-page printed proof which exists in four known copies. One was in the collection of Professor Catel, who used it for his edition. I have been informed that this copy was sold to an American dealer before World War II, but an examination of auction records and extensive correspondence with dealers, libraries, and private collectors have failed to unearth it. Another set is in the Whitman Collection in the Manuscripts Division of the Library of Congress. The third and fourth copies, hereafter referred to as F1 and F2, which will be described in my Introduction, are in the collection of Mr. Charles E. Feinberg of Detroit.

Since F1 and F2 do not necessarily represent Whitman's final intentions, I have adopted the Library of Congress proof sheets, which contain no corrections, as my basic text. Deletions in F1 are enclosed in pointed brackets (<   >) and those in F2 in square brackets. Four insertions in F1 are also in pointed brackets but are noted as insertions.

Even in so slight a task as the making of this edition, one incurs much pleasant indebtedness. I am grateful to the dealers, librarians, and collectors who so kindly replied to my inquiries. Professor Gay Wilson Allen of New York University and Professor Roger Asselineau of the University of Lyon generously shared with me their great knowledge of Whitman. M. Francis Catel of Montpellier very kindly sent me a copy of his father's edition. Mr. T. E. Hanley and Mr. John S. Van E. Kohn gave me leads, for which I am grateful. The University of Kansas Libraries procured photostats for me, and the Regents of the University, by a research grant, made possible part of my work. The Editor of the University of Kansas Press has made many helpful suggestions. My greatest debt, however, is to Mr. Charles E. Feinberg, who very generously supplied photostats of his two sets of proofs and has answered many questions.

CONTENTS

INTRODUCTION

"The Eighteenth Presidency!" expresses Whitman's response to the furious controversy of the campaign summer of 1856. The presidential election of that year was fought primarily over the question of whether slavery should be extended into the recently formed territories of Nebraska and Kansas: a decision which had been left to the settlers by the Kansas-Nebraska Bill of 1854. Concerning the complicated question of the Bill, it is sufficient to point out that not only the transference of such a decision from Congress to the people of the territories but also the loosely drawn terms of the Bill created a most serious Constitutional problem and aggravated the slavery controversy, which had disrupted the moral, economic, and political unity of the nation for thirty-five years. A short summary of events, however, may help make clear the cause of the political frenzy of 1856. After the passage of the Kansas-Nebraska Bill in 1854, Kansas had become the scene of guerrilla warfare between free-soil and pro-slavery settlers. The latter were assisted by border ruffians from Missouri, who posed as legitimate settlers at elections and raided free-soilers at other times. They also had the great advantage of support from the territorial government, which was pro-slavery. The free-soilers, while less formidable than their opponents, received moral and political support from free-soil advocates in the North and East. Modern students of the Kansas Crisis agree

[1]

that legend drew too lurid a picture of "bleeding Kansas," but it was legend which inflamed minds in 1856 and the facts themselves were bad enough. In October, 1855, the free-soil settlers had repudiated the fraudulently elected territorial legislature and had written a constitution for submission to Congress. In February, 1856, Charles Robinson was elected governor by the free-soilers, and at the end of the winter, active violence began again. During April, May, and June, against the background of inflammatory reports from the territory, Congress debated the Kansas question. In May the House sent a committee to investigate the troubles on the spot. On May 21, shortly after the arrival of the committee in Lawrence, the principal free-soil settlement, a sheriff's posse raided and sacked the town and arrested several free-soil leaders for treason. Charles Robinson, who had left for the East on a mission, had already, on the 20th, been arrested at Lexington, Missouri, and taken back to Kansas, where he was held at Lecompton on the charge of treason. In Washington, on the 20th, Charles Sumner, the hero of the abolitionists, concluded his vituperative speech to the Senate, "The Crime against Kansas." On the 22nd Representative Preston Brooks of South Carolina brutally clubbed Sumner in his seat in the Senate for offensive personalities directed against Brooks's uncle, Senator Andrew Butler. A few days later, at the height of the excitement over this attack, the news of the raid on Lawrence and Robinson's imprisonment reached the newspapers of the East. The news of John Brown's murder and mutilation of five pro-slavery settlers on Pottawatomie Creek on the night of the 25th and 26th arrived a few days later, but received much less attention in the Northern papers. But even before the events just described, the sectional struggle had become so intense as to shatter the major political parties. A new party had been formed by dissident Whigs and Democrats and by former members of the old Free-Soil party. As a result in 1856 there were three major candidates: Millard Fillmore for the Whigs and Americans (Know-Nothings), James Buchanan for the Democrats, and John Charles Frémont, hero of Rocky Mountain explorations, for the Republicans.

Although "The Eighteenth Presidency!" is concerned with the bankruptcy of party politics, it touches on most of the issues of the campaign and of the underlying situation. Yet it is not a party tract, for Whitman had his own point of view. Although he believed that slavery was undemocratic, he was not an Abolitionist. He was never, in fact, completely sympathetic with the slave. He felt, for example, that the Negro was better off under slavery than in his native freedom and, for that matter, better off than the free European laborer. The crime of slavery was a crime against democracy, not against the slave, and few minor inconsistencies in Whitman's opinions are more striking than that represented by his statements about slaves and slavery in his newspaper prose and those in his poetry. His principal concern as a journalist in the late 1840's and early 1850's was with the spread of slavery beyond the borders of the South. As a workingman and the son of a workingman, he was quick to see a possible threat to the free white farmer or workman. For these reasons he shared the Republican sense of outrage at the Kansas policy of the outgoing Democratic administration even though, as we shall see, he was probably not a Republican in 1856.

But though he abhorred the Slave Power he did not wish to split the Union. The passionate outcry of "The Eighteenth Presidency!" arises from his perception that the cynicism, ineptitude, and lack of vision of politicians of all parties were leading to a sectional split. Whitman was a nationalist, not in any chauvinistic fashion, but in his deep love of the Union. This aspect of his thought has often been overshadowed in the minds of his readers by his patriotic pride in his country and by his passion for democratic equalitarianism. Actually, for him national unity and equalitarianism were almost one. Without the union of "These States," democracy would cease to exist. Therefore, although "The Eighteenth Presidency!" can be carelessly read as an antislavery tract or as a Republican document, its principal purpose is to preserve the Union by a reform of the political system.

"The Eighteenth Presidency!" is the last important statement of Whitman's early nationalism. Like the great senatorial antagonists, Webster and Calhoun, he argues the case legalistically, although, being a radical, he does not hesitate to invoke the "higher law" of the Declaration of Independence. Yet within a score of months, in the "Calamus" poems he began to extol "love of Comrades" as the strongest nationalistic tie. The poems of the 1855 edition revealed an anomalous inner life, but it is only in the poems written after 1856 that this life becomes rationalized into a political philosophy. Meanwhile, as he had in the columns of the Brooklyn *Eagle,* he argued the case for national union in the traditional terms of the social-compact theory.

Whitman had read an abridgment of Rousseau's *Social Contract,* but, even if he had not, he could scarcely have escaped knowing something about the compact theory, for it was the orthodox theory of his day. But his use of it goes beyond traditional limits. His admiration for the Constitution, the great national compact, knew no bounds. It was to him "a perfect and entire thing." It is to the Constitution that he appealed for the solution of the problems of 1856. Yet it was not the only compact which he venerated. Even higher than the Constitution stood the Declaration of Independence, the "primary compact." There were still more compacts, and it becomes obvious that the word "compact" had for him only a metaphorical meaning. If the national compacts include "the action of the earlier Congresses, the spirit of the fathers and warriors, the official lives of Washington, Jefferson, Madison," clearly he was appealing to the democratic tradition as symbolized or stated in historical acts and documents, a tradition which he knew (despite his legalism) to be stronger than any formal agreement.

The solution he proposed seemed to him to meet the demands of the crisis within the terms of the various American compacts. He believed that slavery was repugnant to American ideals, but that since the Constitution sanctioned it, it must be left where it existed.

He also demanded that the North meet its Constitutional obligation to return fugitive slaves. Yet he was aware that the Constitution is not immutable but dynamic. Therefore he insisted that it be interpreted in the light of the advanced moral sentiment of his day. If slavery must be protected where the Constitution permitted it, it must not be allowed to spread to the new territories. To him this was not a question to be settled by citation of precedents or interpretations of the Compromise of 1850. It was a question of moral right or wrong.

As for party affiliation, Whitman was taking a position somewhere between the attitudes of the Whigs and Democrats and that of the Republicans. The older parties were willing to conciliate the South in order to preserve the Union (and themselves) at all costs. Slavery was not a moral issue to them, but rather a factor which had to be taken into account in political calculation. No solid thinker among them could take the affirmations of the Declaration of Independence seriously as a philosophy for political action, least of all for action on the slavery question. Rufus Choate, the great Whig lawyer, in August of 1856, denounced "the glittering and sounding generalities of the Declaration of Independence." The Republican party was not an abolition party; it denied the frequently made charge that it was a disunionist party, but it was intransigent on the free-soil issue. Therefore it seemed impossible for any political party to settle the Kansas issue while preserving the Union.

Whitman therefore turned to what he somewhat naïvely considered a nonpolitical solution. As he saw it, the chief barrier to the restoration of national unity and the containment of slavery was the political parties. The government, he vehemently insisted, had been stolen from the people by the professional politicians, North and South, whose eyes were only on profit and power. In the North were the corrupt jobsters, in the South the 350,000 slaveholders. In both sections the people had been deceived by an evil minority. The nomination of Buchanan and Fillmore was only a climax of political cynicism. Whitman therefore proposed the abolition of all parties. The paragraph he addressed to Frémont, while not hostile, is not an endorsement but a warning. In place of parties he proposed a working-class youth movement. North, South, East, and West, the young workingmen were to repudiate parties and take the leadership to which they were destined by the American tradition, not to overthrow the Union but to maintain it.

The idea of mobilizing the young workingmen was not new in Whitman's thinking, nor was he the only liberal to perceive the possibilities in the younger voters. The Republicans were attempting to mobilize them behind Frémont, who was only forty-three years old. Whitman himself, after the Compromise of 1850, had called on the young men in "Wounded in the House of Friends": "Arise young North! / Our elder blood flows in the veins of cowards." The audience to which his poetry is addressed is the young men and women. The idea of a working-class democracy had been instilled in him in childhood, for his father had been a member of the working-class wing of the Democrats in Brooklyn. In 1831 the elder Whitman got a job for his son in the printing office of the Long Island *Patriot,* a paper to which he subscribed. One of the favorite slogans of the *Patriot* had been "The right of the people to rule in every case." This slogan might well have been printed on the masthead of the Brooklyn *Eagle* during Whitman's editorship. The idea of working-class democracy appears in his poetry also, for, although he theoretically refused to exclude anyone from brotherhood, on examination it appears that he usually equated "man" with "workingman."

Since Whitman was an experienced political journalist, it is almost incredible that he could have thought that political parties could be abolished. Indeed the party system had developed in Whitman's own lifetime in answer to a Constitutional need. There is no direct evidence to show that Whitman was familiar with the hostility to "factions" felt by the Founding Fathers. At least he never appealed to them as a precedent on this point. Although Whitman was affected by the contemporary predilection for a government of restricted powers, he was not a philosophical anarchist. He always revered the Constitution.

Yet his attitude is not inexplicable. In 1856 he was still gripped by his role as prophet of democracy, and practical considerations were of little significance to him. Furthermore, his experience with parties had been as unfortunate as it had been close, for in 1848 his free-soil politics had lost him the editorship of the *Eagle* and caused him to break with the Democratic party. But he had been a delegate that same year to the Free Soil convention which nominated Martin Van Buren and Charles Francis Adams. Late in life he said that he had voted for John P. Hale, the Free Soil party candidate in 1852, and that he had voted for Lincoln.[1] It would have been consistent to vote with the Republicans in 1856. But it is quite possible that he did not. Despite the fact that the Republican party was composed of antislavery Whigs, former members of the old Free Soil party, and free-soil Democrats, there is some evidence that the old radical Democrats were uneasy in their alliance with the Whigs in the cause of freedom. Certainly, aside from its free-soil plank, the Republican platform was a Whig platform, and Whitman had grown up a radical Jacksonian Democrat in the days of the Bank War. Moreover, Frémont was an abolitionist, and Whitman was not. Whitman may or may not have voted for Lincoln in 1860. At least I doubt it, for in 1858 and 1859 he had been expressing fervent admiration for Stephen A. Douglas. But his specific comment on Frémont in "The Eighteenth Presidency!" (page 39) and his hostility toward political parties seem certain evidence that he did not vote the Republican ticket in 1856. Probably he did not vote at all. The year 1856 seems to have permanently disillusioned him with parties. Later in life he was a nominal Republican, but his general attitude was that of detachment. As for the impracticability of his repudiation of political parties in 1856, one can only say that this is the strain of weakness in his magnificent idealism.

Another source of interest in "The Eighteenth Presidency!" is its relationship to Whitman's poetry, which is the expression of his idealism. Whitman's first volume had appeared in 1855, and in the spring and summer of 1856 while he was writing "The Eighteenth Presidency!" he was preparing the second edition of *Leaves of Grass,* which was published on September 1. At first the differences between the tract and the poems seem more striking than the relationships, for the predominant tone of the 1856 edition of the *Leaves,* like that of the 1855 edition, is lyrical, and its statement is private. The theme is self-discovery. "The Eighteenth Presidency!" is declamatory and public. The poems indeed do concern America, but despite the realism of the catalogues and the genre sketches, the America described in the poems is spiritual rather than political or historical. Democracy is symbolized in the poems rather than discussed. Whitman seems in fact to have avoided as far as possible the composition of poetry overtly on public issues. Yet there are direct relationships between the tract and the poems of 1855 and 1856. I have already commented on Whitman's interest in the young workingman. In the 1855 *Leaves,* "A Boston Ballad—1854" and the moving descriptions of Negroes, especially of fugitive slaves ("Song of Myself," sections 10, 13, 33), are related to his disgust at the Fugitive Slave Act of 1850, which he denounces on other grounds in the tract (page 38). The new poems of 1856 parallel a little more explicitly the statements of "The Eighteenth Presidency!" The general spirit of the bitter "Poem of the Propositions of Nakedness" is that of disgust at the degradation of American life. Line 4 of "Poem of Remembrance for a Girl or Boy of These States" is virtually identical with a sentence on the Declaration of Independence in the tract (page 35). Section 5 of "Song of the Broad-Axe" asserts the right of the common man to rule. The new internationalism of "Salut au Monde" possibly springs from Whitman's dislike of the Know-Nothings (page 30) and suggests the conclusion of "The Eighteenth Presidency!" Even in the 1860 edition of the *Leaves* one finds bitter or anguished references to the preceding four years. A number of these were later dropped, but among those retained are the scornful "To a President" and "To the States, To Identify the 16th, 17th, and 18th Presidentiads."[2] Whitman was troubled by many things, personal and poetical, between 1855 and 1861, but one is tempted to give his political agony the position of first importance, for it was not until the earliest "Drum-Taps" poems of 1861 that the anguished tone of the 1856-1860 poems is abandoned.

Perhaps the most important relationship in thought between "The Eighteenth Presidency!" and Whitman's poems is that between the spiritual nationalism of the poems and the political nationalism of the tract. As I have said, Whitman believed that a split in the national Union would imperil democracy. He never thought that democracy had been completely achieved in the United States—his poems were intended to help bring about complete democracy—but he did believe that the ultimate perfection of democracy depended upon the perpetuation of the Union. To adopt his words of 1871 in *Democratic Vistas,* he considered "Democracy" and "America" as convertible terms. Therefore, if Union is not preached directly in the early poems, it is dramatized there in

[11]

the symbolic person of the poet, who represents America en masse. As he says in "Song of Myself" (sections 16, 31):

> I am of young and old, of the foolish as much as
>   the wise. . .
> A Southerner soon as a Northerner, a planter non-
>   chalant and hospitable down by the Oconee I
>   live. . .
> Of every hue and caste am I, of every rank and re-
>   ligion . . . .
> I find I incorporate gneiss, coal, long-threaded
>   moss, fruits, grains, esculent roots,
> And am stucco'd with quadrupeds and birds all
>   over. . . .

The reference here is personal, and Whitman's self-identification with the "planter nonchalant and hospitable" is only one of a series of identifications, but American national unity is implicit in the process of "merging" which he is describing here. The union of the early poems is a cosmic union of life through time and space. It resembles the cosmic unity of nature, and its political aspect in Whitman's thought is the union of "These States."

There are also significant relationships in literary form between "The Eighteenth Presidency!" and the poems. Although "The Eighteenth Presidency!" is a tract, not only Whitman's use of direct and rhetorical question and reply but also his sentence rhythms suggest that he was thinking in the patterns of oratory rather than those of the essay or editorial. Much of his verse has an oratorical quality, and he often referred to himself as an orator as well as a bard or poet.

He was not certain for many years just what form his prophetic mission was to take, and almost to the end of his life oratory appealed to him as an alternate form to poetry. In the eighteen-fifties he was especially interested in oratory. His brother George later said that during the 'fifties Whitman wrote "barrels" of lectures. His early notes are full of discussions of oratory. Equally significant is the bombastic open letter to Emerson in the 1856 *Leaves*: "I much enjoy making poems. Other work have I set for myself to do, to meet people and the States face to face, to confront them with an American rude tongue: but the work of my life is making poems. . . . In poems and speeches will I say the word that has got to be said." In 1858 he drew up a prospectus for such speeches. "The Eighteenth Presidency!" is "the Voice of Walt Whitman to each Young Man in the Nation, North, South, East, and West." He seeks to "initiate my name, Walt Whitman," among the workingmen. Out of this same urge to oratory grew the last ten sections of "Song of Myself," "Song of the Open Road," and "Salut au Monde!" "The Eighteenth Presidency!" is not poetry written as prose, like the 1855 Preface; for one thing it lacks the imagery of the Preface. But the manner of the tract, and even details of style like lists of cities (page 41), the lists of occupations, and the epithets in series, which suggest the poetic catalogues, are reminiscent of *Leaves of Grass*.

Although few people would agree with Amy Lowell that "The Eighteenth Presidency!" is *"la plus belle page de Whitman,"*[3] the tract is not contemptible. Its faults are, of course, obvious. Even though he was a great poet, Whitman was often a poor stylist, and his prose is always clumsy. The awkward sentences, inept diction, and bathetic patriotism of "The Eighteenth Presidency!" are familiar horrors to readers of his prose and poetry, especially that in which he was making, as F. O. Matthiessen put it, "a frontal assault on 'Democracy, ma femme.' " Yet there is much to be said for the tract. In one of his notes on oratory, Whitman pictured himself as delivering an antislavery address: "an oration of liberty—up-braiding, full of invective—with enthusiasm."[4] He might well have been talking about "The Eighteenth Presidency!," for passionate energy is its chief characteristic. Furthermore it is Whitman's most carefully organized prose work. It is of course far less complex than the relentlessly logical structure of Calhoun's speeches or the elaborately rhetorical pattern of Webster's, but it is in the same tradition. His pattern is a simple one, but it is effective for his purposes.

A date of composition for "The Eighteenth Presidency!" cannot be precisely assigned. The context indicates the summer of 1856, a date which is confirmed by Whitman's note, "written & printed summer of 1856," on F1. The earliest likely date would be after the middle of June, by which time the conventions had nominated the candidates. The latest possible date of composition is mid-September, for Charles Robinson (see pages 2 and 25) was released from prison then. It has always been assumed that "The Eighteenth Presidency!" was printed in proofs but never

published, but the discovery of Whitman's note on
F1 raises the possibility that he did find a publisher
somewhere. The printer of the proofs, of course, cannot be identified, although a good guess would be that
it was the Rome Brothers of Brooklyn, who printed
the 1855 *Leaves* and did odd printing jobs for Whitman as late as 1872.[5] The tract is too short for pam-
phlet publication, but of suitable length for the newspapers of the day. The three newspapers most likely
to have accepted such a contribution from Whitman
in 1856 were the Brooklyn *Daily Times,* the New
York *Evening Post,* and the New York *Tribune.* A
search of these three papers (including the weekly
Tribune) for the period from June 1 through Election Day has disclosed no published version of "The
Eighteenth Presidency!" This, however, is not sur-
prising, for, since the *Post* and the *Tribune* were en-
thusiastically supporting Frémont, they would hardly
have cared to print a contribution which was hostile
to all political parties and was less than lukewarm toward their hero. The *Daily Times* was much less fervent in its support of Frémont, but it had far less avail-
able space than the great New York dailies and was
primarily interested in Brooklyn affairs. Therefore,
when Whitman wrote "printed" on F1, he must have
meant nothing more than that the proofs had been
printed in 1856. He may have sent copies to editors
and rich men, but probably none of them paid any attention to it.

Clearly, although Whitman did not place "The
Eighteenth Presidency!" among his collected works,

it was more to him than an ephemeral tract. The revisions on F1 and F2, which I shall discuss shortly, are evidence of that. The parallels of thought and style between the tract and his other writings indicate that he was dealing with a matter of deep personal significance. It seems probable that even the degeneration of the presidency had been on his mind, for at some time before 1856 he had thought of writing a poem to review "past presidentiads" to show that "this nation makes as great use of shallow Presidents as of its brave and just Washington, or its wise Jefferson."[6]

Whitman's later use of the tract equally demonstrates his interest in it, for, even if it failed to find an audience in its original form, Whitman kept it in mind, in accordance with his usual habit of salvaging discarded material whenever possible. In 1874 he used the description of workingmen entering "Congress and other official stations" and of the workingman President (pages 20-21) in "Rulers Strictly out of the Masses."[7] The next year he used two paragraphs in which he described the characters and hangouts of contemporary politicians (pages 28-29) in *Memoranda during the War* and in "The American War" in the London *Examiner*.[8] In 1879 he used a sentence on the lessons of the sixteenth and seventeenth presidencies (page 23) in "The Death of Abraham Lincoln."[9] In 1882 he used this and other passages (pages 23-24, 26-27) in "Origins of Attempted Secession."[10] Having thus used relevant sections of "The Eighteenth Presidency!" as he needed them, there was no point in his including it in *Complete Prose Works* (1882).

Both F1 and F2 are heavily revised. Both contain deletions in red ink and black pencil. F1 has two insertions in pencil and the note in the upper left-hand corner of the first sheet in Whitman's hand in ink: "written & printed summer of 1856." F2 contains certain indecipherable marks at the extreme lower left edge of the first page, which appear to have been made with a broad-nibbed pen, or are possibly blottings from another paper. They do not seem to have any connection with the text, whereas the corrections on F1 are connected to the text by guide lines. Both sets are two pages in length. Since the lineage of both F1 and F2 is indisputable, there is no reason to question the authenticity of the changes.

The use of both ink and pencil on both F1 and F2 suggests at least two reworkings of each proof, but there is no way either of establishing the priority of the corrections on any one proof or establishing which proof is the later. Obviously, however, Whitman worked over the tract with his usual care. It is also difficult to come to any conclusion about the significance of the changes, although two hypotheses have been tested. (1) Since Whitman sometimes used proofs in the intermediate stages of poetic revision, both proofs may represent steps in the preparation of final printer's copy in 1856. But the heavy deletions in F2 remove what would seem to be important material —for example, the paragraphs on the return of runaway slaves and the paragraph addressed to Frémont (page 39). The deletions on F1 might have been to improve the style. (2) The changes may represent revisions for a possible printing after 1856. For example, in F1, the insertion of "and 18th" (page 23) clearly suggests that Whitman was thinking of 1860. But if Whitman was planning to use F1 in 1860, why did he not remove the references to Frémont, who was not an important candidate in 1860, and the denunciations of Buchanan and Fillmore? The heavy deletions on F2 suggest plans for use in 1860, yet references to Buchanan and Fillmore still stand. In short, the intention behind the changes is impenetrable except for the insertion of "and 18th" in F1. Some of the deletions on F1 (pages 23-24) are probably for the purpose of improving the style. Other than this, no hypothesis fits all the evidence.

THE EIGHTEENTH PRESIDENCY!

Voice of Walt Whitman to each Young Man in the Nation, North, South, East, and West.

First, Who are the Nation?

Before the American era, the programme of the classes of a nation read thus, first the king, second the noblemen and gentry, third the great mass of mechanics, farmers, men following the water, and all laboring persons. The first and second classes are unknown to the theory of the government of These States; the likes of the class rated third on the old programme were intended to be, and are in fact, and to all intents and purposes, the American nation, the people.

Mechanics, farmers, sailors, &c., constitute some six millions of the inhabitants of These States; merchants, lawyers, doctors, teachers, and priests, count up as high as five hundred thousand; the owners of slaves number three hundred and fifty thousand; the population of The States being altogether about thirty millions, seven tenths of whom are women and children.[11] At present, the personnel of the government of these thirty millions, in executives and elsewhere, is drawn from limber-tongued lawyers, very

[19]

fluent but empty, feeble old men, professional politicians, dandies, dyspeptics, and so forth, and rarely drawn from the solid body of the people; the effects now seen, and more to come. Of course the fault, if it be a fault, is for reasons, and is of the people themselves, and will mend when it should mend.

HAS MUCH BEEN DONE IN THE THEORY OF THESE STATES?

Very good; more remains. Who is satisfied with the theory, or a parade of the theory? I say, delay not, come quickly to its most courageous facts and illustrations. I say no body of men are fit to make Presidents, Judges, and Generals, unless they themselves supply the best specimens of the same, and that supplying one or two such specimens illuminates the whole body for a thousand years.

I expect to see the day when the like of the present personnel of the governments, federal, state, municipal, military, and naval, will be looked upon with derision, and when qualified mechanics and young men will reach Congress and other official stations, sent in their working costumes, fresh from their benches and tools, and returning to them again with dignity. The young fellows must prepare to do credit to this destiny, for the stuff is in them. Nothing gives place, recollect, and never ought to give place except to its clean superiors. There is more rude and undeveloped bravery, [friendship,][12] conscientiousness, [clear-sightedness,] and practical genius for any scope of action, even the broadest and highest, now among the American mechanics and young men, than in all the

[20]

official persons in These States, legislative, executive, judicial, military, and naval, and more than among all the literary persons. I would be much pleased to see some heroic, shrewd, [fully-informed,] healthy-bodied, [middle-aged, beard-faced] American blacksmith or boatman come down from the West across the Alleghanies, and walk into the Presidency, dressed in a clean suit of working attire, and with the tan all over his face, breast, and arms; I would certainly vote for that sort of man, possessing the due requirements, before any other candidate. Such is the thought that must become familiar to you, whoever you are, and to the people of These States; and must eventually take shape in action.

At present, we are environed with nonsense under the name of respectability. Everywhere lowers that stifling atmosphere that makes all the millions of farmers and mechanics of These States the helpless supple-jacks of a comparatively few politicians. Somebody must make a bold push. The people, credulous, generous, deferential, allow the American government to be managed in many respects as is only proper under the personnel of a king and hereditary lords; or, more truly, not proper under any decent men anywhere. If this were to go on, we ought to change the title of the President, and issue patents of nobility. Of course it is not to go on; the Americans are no fools. I perceive meanwhile that nothing less than marked inconsistencies and usurpations will arouse a nation, and make ready for better things afterwards.

<But what ails the present Way of filling the
Offices of The States? Is it not good enough?>[13]

<I should say it was not.> <Result to-day, of?>[14]
To-day of all the persons in public office in These
States, not one in a thousand has been chosen by any
spontaneous movement of the people, nor is attend-
ing to the interests of the people; all have been nominated and put through by great or small caucuses of
the politicians, or appointed as rewards for election-
eering; and all consign themselves to personal and
party interests. Neither in the Presidency, nor in Congress, nor in the foreign ambassadorships, nor in the
governorships of The States, nor in legislatures, nor
in the mayoralities of cities, nor the aldermanships,
nor among the police, nor on the benches of judges,
do I observe a single bold, muscular, young, well-in-
formed, well-beloved, resolute American man, bound
to do a man's duty, aloof from all parties, and with
a manly scorn of all parties. Instead of that, every
trustee of the people is a traitor, looking only to his
own gain, and to boost up his party. The berths, the
Presidency included, are bought, sold, electioneered
for, prostituted, and filled with prostitutes. In the
North and East, swarms of dough-faces,[15] office-ver-
min, kept-editors, clerks, attaches of the ten thousand
officers and their parties, aware of nothing further
than the drip and spoil of politics—ignorant of principles, the true glory of a man. In the South, no end of
blusterers, braggarts, windy, melodramatic, contin-
ually screaming in falsetto, a nuisance to These States,
their own just as much as any; altogether the most im-

pudent persons that have yet appeared in the history of lands, and with the most incredible successes, having pistol'd, bludgeoned, yelled and threatened America, the past twenty years into one long train of cowardly concessions, and still not through, but rather at the commencement. Their cherished secret scheme is to dissolve the union of These States.[16]

<WELL, WHAT MORE?>

Is nothing but breed upon breed like these to be represented in the Presidency? Are parties to forever usurp the government? Are lawyers, dough-faces, and the three hundred and fifty thousand owners of slaves, to sponge the mastership of thirty millions? Where is the real America? Where are the laboring persons, ploughmen, men with axes, spades, scythes, flails? Where are the carpenters, masons, machinists, drivers of horses, workmen in factories? Where is the spirit of the manliness and common-sense of These States? It does not appear in the government. It does not appear at all in the Presidency.

LESSON OF THE SIXTEENTH AND SEVENTEENTH TERMS OF THE PRESIDENCY.

The sixteenth and seventeenth <and 18th>[17] terms of the American Presidency have shown that the villainy and shallowness of great rulers are just as eligible to These States as to any foreign despotism, kingdom, or empire—there is not a bit of difference. History is to record these two Presidencies[18] as so far our topmost warning and shame. Never were publicly

[23]

displayed more deformed, mediocre, snivelling, unreliable, false-hearted men! Never were These States so insulted, and attempted to be betrayed! All the main purposes for which the government was established are openly denied. The perfect equality of slavery with freedom is flauntingly preached in the North—nay, the superiority of slavery. The slave trade is proposed to be renewed.[19] Everywhere frowns and misunderstandings—everywhere exasperations and humiliations. The President eats dirt <and excrement> for his daily meals, <likes it,> and tries to force it on The States. The cushions of the Presidency are nothing but filth <and blood>. The pavements of Congress are <also> bloody. <The land that flushed amazed at the basest outrage of our times, grows pale with a far different feeling to see the outrage unanimously commended back again to those who only half rejected it.> The national tendency toward populating the territories full of free work-people, established by the organic compacts of These States, promulged by the fathers, the Presidents, the old warriors, and the earlier Congresses, a tendency vital to the life and thrift of the masses of the citizens, is violently put back under the feet of slavery, and against the free people the masters of slaves are everywhere held up by the President,[20] by the red hand. In fifteen of The States the three hundred and fifty thousand masters keep down the true people, the millions of white citizens, mechanics, farmers, boatmen, manufacturers, and the like, excluding them from politics and from office, and punishing by the lash, by tar and feathers, binding fast to rafts on the rivers or trees in the woods, and sometimes by death, all attempts to discuss the evils of slavery in its relations to the whites. The people of the territories are denied the power to form State governments unless they consent to fasten upon them the slave-hopple, the iron wristlet, and the neck-spike. For refusing such consent, the governor and part of the legislature of the State of Kansas are chased, seized, chained, by the creatures of the President, and are to-day in chains.[21] Over the vast continental tracts of unorganized American territory, equal in extent to all the present organized States, and in future to give the law to all, the whole executive, judicial, military and naval power of These States is forsworn to the people, the rightful owners, and sworn to the help of the three hundred and Fifty [sic] thousand masters of slaves, to put them through this continent, with their successors, at their pleasure, and to maintain by force their mastership over their slave men and women, slave-farmers, slave-miners, slave-blacksmiths, slave-carpenters, slave-cartmen, slave-sailors, and the like. Slavery is adopted as an American institution, superior, national, constitutional, right in itself, and under no circumstances to take any less than freedom takes. Nor is that all; to-day, to-night, the constables and commissioners of the President can by law step into any part of These States and pick out whom they please, deciding which man or woman they will allow to be free, and which shall be a slave, no jury to intervene, but the commissioner's mandate to be enforced by the federal troops and cannon, and has been actually so enforced.[22]

[25]

⟨ARE THE STATES⟩ ⟨IS LIBERTY—IS PROGRESS⟩[23] RETARDED THEN?

No; while all is drowned and desperate that the government has had to do with, all outside the influence of government, (for ever the largest part,) thrives and smiles. The sun shines, corn grows, men go merrily about their affairs, houses are built, ships arrive and depart. Through evil and through good, the republic stands, and is for centuries yet to stand, immovable from its foundations. No, no; out of dastards and disgraces, fortunate are the wrongs that call forth stout and angry men; then is shown what stuff there is in a nation.

The young genius of America is not going to be emasculated and strangled just as it arrives toward manly age. It shall live, and yet baffle the politicians and the three hundred and fifty thousand masters of slaves.

NOMINEES OF THE POLITICIANS.

Now the term of the seventeenth Presidency passing hooted and spurned to its close, the delegates of the politicians have nominated for the eighteenth term, Buchanan of Pennsylvania, and Fillmore of New York, separate tickets, but men both patterned to follow and match the seventeenth term, both disunionists, both old politicians, both sworn down to the theories of special parties, and of all others the theories that balk and reverse the main purposes of the founders of These States. Such are the nominees that have arisen out of the power of the politicians; but another power has also arisen.

COUNTERACTION OF A NEW RACE OF YOUNG MEN.

A new race copiously appears, with resolute tread, soon to confront Presidents, Congresses and parties, to look them sternly in the face, to stand no nonsense; American young men, the offspring and proof of These States, the West the same as the East, and the South alike with the North.

America sends these young men in good time, for they were needed. Much waits to be done. First, people need to realize who are poisoning the politics of These States.

<WHENCE T><T>²⁴HE DELEGATES OF THE POLITICIANS <?> WHENCE THE BUCHANAN AND FILLMORE CONVENTIONS?

Not from sturdy American freemen; not from industrious homes; not from thrifty farms; not from the ranks of fresh-bodied young men; not from among teachers, poets, savans [sic], learned persons, beloved persons, temperate persons; not from among ship-builders, engineers, agriculturists, scythe-swingers, corn-hoers; <not from the race of mechanics;> not from that great strong stock of Southerners that supplied the land in old times; not from the real West, the log-hut, the clearing, the woods, the prairie, the hill-side; not from the sensible, generous, rude Californian miners; nor from the best specimens of Massachusetts, Maine, New Jersey, Pennsylvania, Ohio, Illinois, Wisconsin, Indiana, nor from the untainted unpolitical citizens of the cities.

[27]

WHENCE THEN DO THESE NOMINATING DICTATORS OF AMERICA YEAR AFTER YEAR START OUT?

From lawyers' offices, secret lodges, back-yards, bed-houses, and bar-rooms; from out of the custom-houses, marshals' offices, post-offices, and gambling hells; from the President's house, the jail, the venereal hospital, the station-house; from unnamed by-places where devilish disunion is hatched at midnight; from political hearses, and from the coffins inside, and from the shrouds inside of the coffins; from the tumors and abscesses of the land; from the skeletons and skulls in the vaults of the federal almshouses; from the running sores of the great cities; thence to the national, state, city, and district nominating conventions of These States, come the most numerous and controlling delegates.

WHO ARE THEY PERSONALLY?

Office-holders, office-seekers, robbers, pimps, exclusives, malignants, conspirators, murderers, fancy-men, post-masters, custom-house clerks, contractors, kept-editors, spaniels well-trained to carry and fetch, jobbers, infidels, disunionists, terrorists, mail-riflers, slave-catchers, pushers of slavery, creatures of the President, creatures of would-be Presidents, spies, blowers, electioneerers, body-snatchers, bawlers, bribers, compromisers, runaways, lobbyers, sponges, ruined sports, expelled gamblers, policy backers, monte-dealers, duelists, carriers of concealed weapons, blind men, deaf men, pimpled men, scarred inside with the vile disorder, gaudy outside with gold chains made from the people's money and harlot's money twisted together; crawling, serpentine men, the lousy combings and born freedom sellers of the earth.

STRIPT OF PADDING AND PAINT, WHO ARE BUCHANAN AND FILLMORE? WHAT HAS THIS AGE TO DO WITH THEM?

Two galvanized old men, close on the summons to depart this life, their early contemporaries long since gone, only they two left, relics and proofs of the little political bargains, chances, combinations, resentments of a past age, having nothing in common with this age, standing for the first crop of political graves and grave-stones planted in These States, but in no sort standing for the lusty young growth of the modern times of The States. It is clear from all these two men say and do, that their hearts have not been touched in the least by the flowing fire of the humanitarianism of the new world, its best glory yet, and a moral control stronger than all its governments. It is clear that neither of these nominees of the politicians has thus far reached an inkling of the real scope and character of the contest of the day, probably now only well begun, to stretch through years, with varied temporary successes and reverses. Still the two old men live in respectable little spots, with respectable little wants. Still their eyes stop at the edges of the tables of committees and cabinets, beholding not the great round world beyond. What has this age to do with them?

You Americans who travel with such men, or who are nominated on tickets any where with them, or who support them at popular meetings, or write for them in the newspapers, or who believe that any good can come out of them, you also understand not the present age, the fibre of it, the countless currents it brings of American young men, a different superior race. All this effervescence is not for nothing; the friendlier, vaster, more vital modern spirit, hardly yet arrived at definite proportions, or to the knowledge of itself, will have the mastery. The like turmoil prevails in the expressions of literature, manners, trade, and other departments.

To BUTCHERS, SAILORS, STEVEDORES, AND DRIVERS OF HORSES—TO PLOUGHMEN, WOOD-CUTTERS, MARKET-MEN, CARPENTERS, MASONS, AND LABORERS—TO WORKMEN IN FACTORIES—AND TO ALL IN THESE STATES WHO LIVE BY THEIR DAILY TOIL.

Mechanics! A parcel of windy northern liars are bawling in your ears the easily-spoken words Democracy and the democratic party. Others are making a great ado with the word Americanism, a solemn and great word.[25] What the so-called democracy are now sworn to perform would eat the faces off the succeeding generations of common people worse than the most horrible disease. The others are contributing to the like performance, and are using the great word Americanism without yet feeling the first aspiration of it, as the great word Religion has been used, probably loudest and oftenest used, by men that made indiscriminate massacres at night, and filled the world so full with hatreds, horrors, partialities, exclusions, bloody revenges, penal conscience laws and test-oaths. To the virtue of Americanism is happening to-day, what happens many days to many virtues, namely, the masses who possess them but do not understand them are sought to be sold by that very means to those who neither possess them nor understand them. What are the young men suspicious of? I will tell them what it stands them in hand to be suspicious of, and that is American craft; it is subtler than Italian craft; I guess it is about the subtlest craft upon the earth.

What is there in prospect for free farmers and Work people?

A few generations ago, the general run of farmers and work-people like us were slaves, serfs, deprived of their liberty by law; they are still so deprived on some parts of the continent of Europe. To-day, those who are free here, and free in the British islands and else-where, are free through deeds that were done, and men that lived, some of them an age or so ago, and some of them many ages ago. The men and deeds of these days also decide for generations ahead, as past men and deeds decided for us.

As the broad fat States of The West, the largest and best parts of the inheritance of the American farmers and mechanics, were ordained to common people and workmen long in advance by Jefferson, Washington, and the earlier Congresses, now a far[26] ampler west is to be ordained. Is it to be ordained to workmen, or to the masters of workmen? Shall the future mechanics of America be serfs? Shall labor be degraded, and women be whipt in the fields for not performing their tasks? If slaves are not prohibited from all national American territory by law, as prohibited in the beginning, as the organic compacts authorize and require, and if, on the contrary, the entrance and establishment of slave labor through the continent is secured, there will steadily wheel into this Union, for centuries to come, slave state after slave state, the entire surface of the land owned by great proprietors, in plantations of thousands of acres, showing no more sight for free races of farmers and work-people than there is now in any European despotism or aristocracy; and the existence of our present Free States put in jeopardy, because out of that vast territory are to come states enough to overbalance all.

Workmen! Workwomen! Those immense national American tracts belong to you; they are in trust with you; they are latent with the populous cities, numberless farms, herds, granaries, groves, golden gardens, and inalienable homesteads, of your successors. The base political blowers and kept-editors of the North are raising a fog of prevarications around you. But the manlier Southern disunionists, the chieftains among the three hundred and fifty thousand masters, clearly distinguish the issue, and the principle it rests upon. McDuffie, disunionist governor, lays it down with candid boldness that the workingmen of a state are unsafe depositaries of political powers and rights, and that a republic can not permanently exist unless those who ply the mechanical trades and attend to the farm-work are slaves, subordinated by strict laws to their masters.[27] Calhoun, disunionist senator, denounces and denies, in the presence of the world, the main article of the organic compact of These States, that all men are born free and equal, and bequeaths to his followers, at present leaders of the three hundred and fifty thousand masters, guides of the so-called democracy, counsellors of Presidents, and getters-up of the nominations of Buchanan and Fillmore, his deliberate charge, to be carried out against that main article, that it is the most false and dangerous of all political errors; such being the words of that charge, spoken in the summer of the 73d year of These States, and, indeed, carried out since in the spirit of congressional legislation, executive action, and the candidates offered by the political parties to the people.[28]

ARE NOT POLITICAL PARTIES ABOUT PLAYED OUT?

I say they are, all round. America has outgrown parties; henceforth it is too large, and they too small. They habitually make common cause just as soon in advocacy of the worst deeds and men as the best, or probably a little sooner for the worst. I place no reliance upon any old party, nor upon any new party. Suppose one to be formed under the noblest auspices, and getting into power with the noblest intentions, how long would it remain so? How many years? Would it remain so one year? As soon as it becomes successful, and there are offices to be bestowed, the politicians leave the unsuccessful parties, and rush toward it, and it ripens and rots with the rest.

WHAT RIGHT HAS ANY ONE POLITICAL PARTY, NO MATTER WHICH, TO WIELD THE AMERICAN GOVERNMENT?

No right at all. Not the so-called democratic, not abolition, opposition to foreigners, nor any other

[33]

party, should be permitted the exclusive use of the Presidency; and every American young man must have sense enough to comprehend this. I have said the old parties are defunct; but there remains of them empty flesh, putrid mouths, mumbling and squeaking the tones of these conventions, the politicians standing back in shadow, telling lies, trying to delude and frighten the people; and nominating such candidates as Fillmore and Buchanan.

Party Platforms, Sections, Creeds.

What impudence! for any one platform, section, creed, no matter which, to expect to subordinate all the rest, and rule the immense diversity of These free and equal States! Platforms are of no account. The right man is every thing. With the downfall of parties go the platforms they are forever putting up, lowering, turning, repainting, and changing.

The Unchangeable American Platforms.

The platforms for the Presidency of These States are simply the organic compacts of The States, the Declaration of Independence, the Federal Constitution, the action of the earlier Congresses, the spirit of the fathers and warriors, the official lives of Washington, Jefferson, Madison, and the now well-understood and morally established rights of man, wherever the sun shines, the rain falls, and the grass grows.

The Federal Constitution.

Much babble will always be heard in the land about the Federal Constitution, this, that, and the other concerning it. The Federal Constitution is a perfect and entire thing, an edifice put together, not for the accommodation of a few persons, but for the whole human race; not for a day or a year, but for many years, perhaps a thousand, perhaps many thousand. Its architecture is not a single brick, a beam, an apartment, but only the whole. It is the grandest piece of moral building ever constructed; I believe its architects were some mighty prophets and gods. Few appreciate it, Americans just as few as any. Like all perfect works or persons, time only is great enough to give it area. Five or six centuries hence, it will be better understood from results, growths.

The Federal Constitution is the second of the American organic compacts. The premises, outworks, guard, defense, entrance of the Federal Constitution, is the primary compact of These States, sometimes called the Declaration of Independence; and the groundwork, feet, understratum of that again, is its deliberate engagement, in behalf of the States, thenceforward to consider all men to be born free and equal into the world, each one possessed of inalienable rights to his life and liberty, (namely, that no laws passed by any government could be considered to alienate or take away those born rights, the penalties upon criminals being, of course, for the very purpose of preserving those rights.) This is the covenant of the Republic from the beginning, now and forever. It is not a mere opinion; it is the most venerable pledge, with all the forms observed, signed by the commissioners, ratified by The States, and sworn to by Washington at the head of his army, with his hand upon the

[35]

Bible.[29] It is supreme over all American law, and greater than Presidents, Congresses, elections, and what not, for they hurry out of the way, but it remains. Above all, it is carefully to be observed in all that relates to the continental territories. When they are organized into States, it is to be passed over to the good faith of those States.

ONE OR TWO RADICAL PARTS OF THE AMERICAN THEORY OF GOVERNMENT.

Man can not hold property in man. As soon as there are clear-brained original American judges, this saying will be simplified by their judgments, and no State out of the whole confederacy but will confirm and approve those judgments.

Any one of These States is perfect mistress of itself; and each additional State the same. When States organize themselves, the Federal government withdraws, absolved from its duties, except certain specific ones under the Constitution, and only in behalf of them can it interfere in The States.

The true government is much simpler than is supposed, and abstains from much more. Nine tenths of the laws passed every winter at the Federal Capitol, and all the State Capitols, are not only unneeded laws, but positive nuisances, jobs got up for the service of special classes or persons.

Every rational uncriminal person, twenty-one years old, should be eligible to vote, on actual residence, no other requirement needed. The day will come when this will prevail.

The whole American government is itself simply a compact with each individual of the thirty millions of persons now inhabitants of These States, and prospectively with each individual of the hundred millions and five hundred millions that are in time to become inhabitants, to protect each one's life, liberty, industry, acquisitions, without excepting one single individual out of the whole number, and without making ignominious distinctions. Thus is government sublime; thus it is equal; otherwise it is a government of castes, on exactly the same principles with the kingdoms of Europe.

I said the national obligation is passed over to The States. Then if they are false to it, and impose upon certain persons, can the national government interfere? It can not, under any circumstances whatever. We must wait, no matter how long. There is no remedy, except in The State itself. A corner-stone of the organic compacts of America is that a State is perfect mistress of itself. If that is taken away, all the rest may just as well be taken away. When that is taken away, this Union is dissolved.

[MUST RUNAWAY SLAVES BE DELIVERED BACK?]

[They must. Many things have the go-by, but good faith shall never have the go-by.]

[By a section of the fourth article of the Federal Constitution, These States compact each with the other, that any person held to service or labor in one State, under its laws, and escaping into another State, shall not be absolved from service by any law of that other State, but shall be delivered up to the persons to whom such service or labor is due. This part of the second organic compact between the original States should be carried out by themselves in their usual forms, but in spirit and in letter. Congress has no business to pass any law upon the subject, any more than upon the hundred other of the compacts between the States, left to be carried out by their good faith. Why should Congress pick out this particular one? I had quite as lief depend on the good faith of any of These States, as on the laws of Congress and the President. Good faith is irresistible among men, and friendship is; which lawyers can not understand, thinking nothing but compulsion will do.]

But cannot that requirement of the fourth article of the Second Compact be evaded, on any plea whatever, even the plea of its unrighteousness? Nay, I perceive it is not to be evaded on any plea whatever, not even the plea of its unrighteousness. It should be observed by The States, in spirit and in letter, whether it is pleasant to them or unpleasant, beholding in it one item among many items, each of the rest as important as it, and each to be so carried out as not to contravene the rest. As to what is called the Fugitive Slave Law, insolently put over the people by their Congress and President, it contravenes the whole of the organic compacts, and is at all times to be defied in all parts of These States, South or North, by speech, by pen, and, if need be, by the bullet and the sword.]

[Shall we determine upon such things, then, and not leave them to the great judges and the scholars? Yes, it is best that we determine upon such things.]

THE EIGHTEENTH PRESIDENCY!

[TO FREMONT, OF NEW YORK.]

[Whenever the day comes for him to appear, the man who shall be the Redeemer President of These States, is to be the one that fullest realizes the rights of individuals, signified by the impregnable rights of The States, the substratum of this Union. The Redeemer President of These States is not to be exclusive, but inclusive. In both physical and political America there is plenty of room for the whole human race; if not, more room can be provided.]

To THE AMERICAN YOUNG MEN, MECHANICS, FARMERS, BOATMEN, MANUFACTURERS, &C., OF VIRGINIA, DELAWARE, MARYLAND, THE CAROLINAS, KENTUCKY, TENNESSEE, GEORGIA, ALABAMA, FLORIDA, MISSISSIPPI, ARKANSAS, MISSOURI, LOUISIANA AND TEXAS.

How much longer do you intend to submit to the espionage and terrorism of the three hundred and fifty thousand owners of slaves? Are you too their slaves, and their most obedient slaves? Shall no one among you dare open his mouth to say he is opposed to slavery, as a man should be, on account of the whites, and wants it abolished for their sake? Is not a writer, speaker, teacher to be left alive, but those who lick up the spit that drops from the mouths of the three hundred and fifty thousand masters? Is there hardly one free, courageous soul left in fifteen large and populous States? Do the ranks of the owners of slaves themselves contain no men desperate and tired of that service and sweat of the mind, worse than any service in sugar-fields or corn-fields, under the eyes of overseers? Do the three hundred and fifty thousand expect to bar off forever all preachers, poets, philosophers—all that makes the brain of These States, free literature, free thought, the good old cause of liberty? Are they blind? Do they not see those unrelaxed circles of death narrowing and narrowing every hour around them?

You young men of the Southern States! is the word Abolitionist so hateful to you, then? Do you not know that Washington, Jefferson, Madison, and all the great Presidents and primal warriors and sages were declared abolitionists?

You young men! American mechanics, farmers, boatmen, manufacturers, and all work-people of the South, the same as the North! you are either to abolish slavery, or it will abolish you.

To the Three Hundred and Fifty Thousand Owners of Slaves.

Suppose you get Kansas, do you think it would be ended? Suppose you and the politicians put Buchanan into the Eighteenth Presidency, or Fillmore into the Presidency, do you think it would be ended? I know nothing more desirable for those who contend against you than that you should get Kansas. Then would the melt begin in These States that would not cool till Kansas should be redeemed, as of course it would be.

O gentlemen, you do not know whom Liberty has nursed in These States, and depends on in time of need. You have not received any report of the Free

States, but have received only the reports of the trustees who have betrayed the Free States. Do you suppose they will betray many thousand men, and stick at betraying a few men like you? Raised on plantations or in towns full of menial workmen and workwomen, you do not know, as I know, these fierce and turbulent races that fill the Northeast, the East, the West, the Northwest, the Pacific shores, the great cities, Manhattan Island, Brooklyn, Newark, Boston, Worcester, Hartford, New Haven, Providence, Portland, Bangor, Augusta, Albany, Buffalo, Rochester, Syracuse, Lockport, Cleaveland [sic], Detroit, Milwaukee, Racine, Sheboygan, Madison, Galena, Burlington, Iowa City, Chicago, St. Louis, Cincinnati, Columbus, Pittsburgh, Philadelphia, San Francisco, Sacramento, and many more. From my mouth hear the will of These States taking form in the great cities. Where slavery is, there it is. The American compacts, common sense, all things unite to make it the affair of the States diseased with it, to cherish the same as long as they see fit, and to apply the remedy when they see fit. But not one square mile of continental territory shall henceforward be given to slavery, to slaves, or to the masters of slaves—not one square foot. If any laws are passed giving up such territory, those laws will be repealed. In organizing the territories, what laws are good enough for the American freeman must be good enough for you; if you come in under the said laws, well and good; if not, stay away. What is done, is done; henceforth there is no further compromise. All this is now being cast in the stuff that makes the tough national resolves of These States, that every hour only anneals tougher. It is not that putty you see in Congress and in the Presidency; it is iron—it is the undissuadable swift metal of death.

[To Editors of the Independent Press,
and to Rich Persons.]

[Circulate and reprint this Voice of mine for the workingmen's sake. I hereby permit and invite any rich person, anywhere, to stereotype it, or re-produce it in any form, to deluge the cities of The States with it, North, South, East and West. It is those millions of mechanics you want; the writers, thinkers, learned and benevolent persons, merchants, are already secured almost to a man. But the great masses of the mechanics, and a large portion of the farmers, are unsettled, hardly know whom to vote for, or whom to believe. I am not afraid to say that among them I seek to initiate my name, Walt Whitman, and that I shall in future have much to say to them. I perceive that the best thoughts they have wait unspoken, impatient to be put in shape; also that the character, power, pride, friendship, conscience of America have yet to be proved to the remainder of the world.]

The World's Portents, Issues, the 80th Year
of These States.

The times are full of great portents in These States and in the whole world. Freedom against slavery is not issuing here alone, but is issuing everywhere. [The horizon rises, it divides I perceive, for a more august drama than any of the past. Old men have played their parts, the act suitable to them is closed, and if they will not withdraw voluntarily, must be bid to do so with unmistakeable voice. Landmarks of masters, slaves, kings, aristocracies, are moth-eaten, and the peoples of the earth are planting new vast landmarks for themselves. Frontiers and boundaries are less and less able to divide men. The modern inventions, the wholesale engines of war, the world-spreading instruments of peace, the steamship, the locomotive, the electric telegraph, the common newspaper, the cheap book, the ocean mail, are interlinking the inhabitants of the earth together as groups of one family—America standing, and for ages to stand, as the host and champion of the same, the most welcome spectacle ever presented among nations. Every thing indicates unparalleled reforms. Races are marching and countermarching by swift millions and tens of millions. Never was justice so mighty amid injustice; never did the idea of equality erect itself so haughty and uncompromising amid inequality, as to-day. Never were such sharp questions asked as to-day. Never was there more eagerness to know. Never was the representative man more energetic, more like a god, than to-day. He urges on the myriads before him, he crowds them aside, his daring step approaches the arctic and the antarctic poles, he colonizes the shores of the Pacific, the Asiatic Indias, the birthplace of languages and of races, the archipelagoes, Australia; he explores Africa, he unearths Assyria and Egypt, he restates history, he enlarges morality, he speculates anew upon the soul, upon original premises; nothing is left quiet, nothing but he will settle by demonstrations for himself. What whispers are these running through the eastern continents, and crossing the Atlantic and Pacific?] What historic denouements are these we are approaching? On all sides [tyrants tremble, crowns are unsteady,] the human race restive, on the watch for some better era, some divine war. No man knows what will happen next, but all know that some such things are to happen as mark the greatest moral convulsions of the earth. Who shall play the hand for America in these tremendous games? A pretty time to put up two debauched old disunionist politicians, the lees and dregs of more than sixty years! A pretty time for two dead corpses to go walking up and down the earth, to guide by feebleness and ashes a proud, young, friendly, fresh, heroic nation of thirty millions of live and electric men!

NOTES

1. *American Art Association Anderson Galleries, Inc., Manuscripts, Autograph Letters, First Editions and Portraits of Walt Whitman. Formerly the Property of the Late Dr. Richard Maurice Bucke* . . . (New York, 1936), p. 67. The passage is a rejected bit from Bucke's *Walt Whitman* (1883).

2. Written 1858 as "A Past Presidentiad, and one to come also." *Whitman's Manuscripts: Leaves of Grass (1860)*, ed. Fredson Bowers (Chicago, 1955), p. 190.

3. *The Eighteenth Presidency!*, ed. Jean Catel (Montpellier, 1928), p. 3.

4. *Walt Whitman's Workshop*, ed. Clifton Joseph Furness (Cambridge, Mass., 1928), p. 74.

5. *Whitman's Manuscripts: Leaves of Grass (1860)*, p. xxiv.

6. *Complete Writings of Walt Whitman*, IX (New York, 1902), p. 162. Clifton Joseph Furness in *Walt Whitman's Workshop*, p. 277, has called attention to an early draft of the title and first paragraph of "The Eighteenth Presidency!" in *Notes and Fragments* (*Complete Writings, X*, 29), but there seems to be no reason to assume that this draft greatly antedates the writing of the complete tract. In a notebook of the winter of 1855-1856 in the collection of Mr. Charles E. Feinberg are notes on the American party, slavery, the spiritual torpor of the American genius, and the dominance of the 350,000 slave-owners. These may be regarded as early notes towards the finished tract.

7. *Complete Prose Works* (Philadelphia, 1892), p. 334.

8. *Walt Whitman's Workshop*, p. 228, n. 88.

9. *Complete Prose Works*, p. 307.

10. *Ibid.*, pp. 260, 259.

11. Whitman's population figures are askew. In 1850 the occupational distribution of white males over fifteen years of age was, following Whitman's categories: mechanics, farmers, sailors, etc., 5,149,191; professional, 220,665; slaveholders, 347,525. The total population (white, free colored, slaves) was 23,191,876. The occupational distribution is derived from Table LI and the total is from Table X in *The Seventh Census of the United States: 1850* (Washington, 1853), pp. lxxx, xxxi. Although the published census report does not enumerate slaveholders, Whitman's figure agrees with that given by James Ford Rhodes, possibly from Schedule II of the MS census returns. See Rhodes, *History of the United States from the Compromise of 1850*, I (New York, 1892), 345. The number is not given in the printed returns for 1850. I have been unable to discover Whitman's source for the information. In 1860 the total population of the United States was 31,399,301. See *Population of the United States in 1860* [8th Census] (Washington, 1864), p. 597. The number of slaveholders in 1860 was 383,637, according to R. S. Cotterill, *The Old South*, 2nd ed., rev. (Glendale, California, 1939), p. 265.

12. All text in square brackets is deleted in F2 only.

13. All text in pointed brackets is deleted in F1 only. Four insertions in F1 are also in pointed brackets but are noted as insertions. See notes 4, 7, 14, 23 below.

[45]

14. Marginal insertion in F1. Owing to damage to the left edge of the proof, the reading "Result" is conjectural. It was suggested by Mr. Feinberg. The question mark is about three-eighths of an inch to the left of "of." Whitman was apparently questioning a suggested change.

15. An abusive name applied to Northern politicians who sympathized with the South. Although in Whitman's time it was used by Free Soilers and abolitionists, the first citation in *A Dictionary of Americanisms* is from a Southerner, John Randolph of Roanoke, in 1820. See Whitman's "Dough-Face Song" (1850), written as a satire on the Compromise of 1850, *Complete Prose Works*, pp. 339-340.

16. A current charge against the South by Northern radicals, but unjust except as it applied to the extreme fire-eaters, who were no more representative of Southern opinion than was William Lloyd Garrison of Northern. The Southern leaders charged, on the other hand, that the North was driving them into secession; see, for example, Calhoun's "Speech on the Slavery Question," March 4, 1850, in *Works*, ed. R. K. Crallé, V (New York, 1883), 542 ff.

17. Insertion in F1.

18. The administrations of Fillmore and Pierce.

19. As early as 1853 the Charleston *Standard*, supported by the Charleston *Mercury* and the Richmond *Examiner*, had demanded the reopening of the slave trade. After 1855, the topic was regularly discussed at the annual Southern commercial conventions. See Harvey Wish, *George Fitzhugh* (Baton Rouge, 1943), pp. 235-236.

20. Comma inserted by the editor.

21. Whitman's account of events in Kansas is characteristic of the highly colored reporting of such events to be found in the Eastern free-soil press. Robinson's arrest was illegal, but his captors protected him from mob violence and he seems to have been well treated. Certainly he was never chained, and during the summer of 1856 he was in daily and open communication with his free-soil associates.

22. See the denunciation of the Fugitive Slave Act of 1850 in similar terms in *Walt Whitman's Workshop*, pp. 77-81.

23. Marginal insertion in F1.

24. The upper-case "T" is inserted in F1.

25. The American or Know-Nothing party, an outgrowth of earlier nativist and anti-Catholic movements, was organized in 1849 and after 1852 expanded rapidly. It was important in the state and Congressional elections of 1854 and 1855, but split over slavery in 1856. Along with the Whigs, the Northern branch supported Fillmore.

26. End of page 1 of the proof.

27. George McDuffie, 1790-1851, Governor of South Carolina, United States Representative and Senator. The reference is probably to his 1835 message to the legislature of South Carolina. "When these offices [menial labor] are performed by members of the political community, a dangerous element is introduced into the body politic. Hence the alarming tendency to violate the right of property by agrarian legislation which is beginning to be manifest in the older States, where universal suffrage prevails without domestic slavery . . . ."—*American History Leaflets*, ed. Albert Bushnell Hart and Edward Channing, #10 (New York, 1895), 9.

28. John C. Calhoun's "Speech on the Oregon Bill," June 27, 1848. Calhoun was commenting on the proposition that all men are created

equal. "Instead, then, of all men having the same right to liberty and equality . . . liberty is the noblest and highest reward bestowed on mental and moral development, combined with favorable circumstances . . . . The attempt to carry into practice this, the most dangerous of all political errors, and to bestow on all—without regard to their fitness either to acquire or maintain liberty . . . has done more to retard the cause of liberty and civilization, and is doing more at present, than all other causes combined."—*Works*, VI, 511-512.

29. This account is somewhat romanticized. Washington ordered the Declaration read to the Army at New York on July 9 by an aide, he, of course, being present, but there is no evidence that he swore to it on the Bible.